Spotlight

by Buddy Thomas

A Samuel French Acting Edition

New York Hollywood London Toronto

SAMUELFRENCH.COM

Copyright © 2010 by Buddy Thomas

ALL RIGHTS RESERVED

CAUTION: Professionals and amateurs are hereby warned that *SPOTLIGHT* is subject to a Licensing Fee. It is fully protected under the copyright laws of the United States of America, the British Commonwealth, including Canada, and all other countries of the Copyright Union. All rights, including professional, amateur, motion picture, recitation, lecturing, public reading, radio broadcasting, television and the rights of translation into foreign languages are strictly reserved. In its present form the play is dedicated to the reading public only.

The amateur and professional live stage performance rights to *SPOTLIGHT* are controlled exclusively by Samuel French, Inc., and licensing arrangements and performance licenses must be secured well in advance of presentation. PLEASE NOTE that amateur Licensing Fees are set upon application in accordance with your producing circumstances. When applying for a licensing quotation and a performance license please give us the number of performances intended, dates of production, your seating capacity and admission fee. Licensing Fees are payable one week before the opening performance of the play to Samuel French, Inc., at 45 W. 25th Street, New York, NY 10010.

Licensing Fee of the required amount must be paid whether the play is presented for charity or gain and whether or not admission is charged.

Professional/stock licensing fees quoted upon application to Samuel French, Inc.

For all other rights than those stipulated above, apply to: International Creative Management, 825 Eighth Avenue, New York, NY 10019, Attn: Buddy Thomas.

Particular emphasis is laid on the question of amateur or professional readings, permission and terms for which must be secured in writing from Samuel French, Inc.

Copying from this book in whole or in part is strictly forbidden by law, and the right of performance is not transferable.

Whenever the play is produced the following notice must appear on all programs, printing and advertising for the play: "Produced by special arrangement with Samuel French, Inc."

Due authorship credit must be given on all programs, printing and advertising for the play.

ISBN 978-0-573-60072-2   Printed in U.S.A.   #29726

No one shall commit or authorize any act or omission by which the copyright of, or the right to copyright, this play may be impaired.

No one shall make any changes in this play for the purpose of production.

Publication of this play does not imply availability for performance. Both amateurs and professionals considering a production are strongly advised in their own interests to apply to Samuel French, Inc., for written permission before starting rehearsals, advertising, or booking a theatre.

No part of this book may be reproduced, stored in a retrieval system, or transmitted in any form, by any means, now known or yet to be invented, including mechanical, electronic, photocopying, recording, videotaping, or otherwise, without the prior written permission of the publisher.

MUSIC USE NOTE

Licensees are solely responsible for obtaining formal written permission from copyright owners to use copyrighted music in the performance of this play and are strongly cautioned to do so. If no such permission is obtained by the licensee, then the licensee must use only original music that the licensee owns and controls. Licensees are solely responsible and liable for all music clearances and shall indemnify the copyright owners of the play and their licensing agent, Samuel French, Inc., against any costs, expenses, losses and liabilities arising from the use of music by licensees.

IMPORTANT BILLING AND CREDIT REQUIREMENTS

All producers of *SPOTLIGHT must* give credit to the Author of the Play in all programs distributed in connection with performances of the Play, and in all instances in which the title of the Play appears for the purposes of advertising, publicizing or otherwise exploiting the Play and/or a production. The name of the Author *must* appear on a separate line on which no other name appears, immediately following the title and *must* appear in size of type not less than fifty percent of the size of the title type.

CHARACTERS

(All college students – early twenties)

GAIL

BRIAN

MICKEY

KAREN

SETTING

A very messy college dorm room.

TIME

A warm March evening, not long ago……7:30 PM.

*(**AT RISE:** Darkness.)*

(The only shadowy light comes from a few dying rays of sun which have crept in past a drawn window shade.)

(On one bed, there is a hint of passionate movement.... some heavy breathing.)

(Then, all at once, it stops.)

*(**GAIL** sits up and begins fumbling for her clothing.)*

GAIL. Do you know how much I hate rich people? Do you realize how deep and totally overwhelming this hatred is? It's a deep hate. Deep. I want you to know this in case by some astronomical chance I ever come in to a lot of money so you can kick me in the tits in I start displaying symptoms of the wealthy. Symptoms, get it? Cause it's a sickness, a disease that if you're not completely careful makes you forget to be concerned with anyone but yourself, and can I just tell you, Brian, I have no intention of ever being so full of myself and the glamour of the inside of some twelve thousand dollar Prada purse that I forget to notice the rest of the world. I...you know why I'm saying this?

BRIAN. Karen Hedges.

GAIL. *(without stopping from her previous)* It – just – some things really disgust me about this place and it keeps going through my mind about Karen Hedges and how every time there's an audition, her mother mails her American Express Black Card all the way from Phoenix, Arizona, to little Miss Karen, who is then at full liberty to take that card, black, it's BLACK, ok, that means that only like billionaires have them, and Karen's allowed to charge whatever dress she wants to wear to the audition, no matter the price, no matter the place, no matter. Whatever dress. Whatever! You get it? It's not a problem. She can do it. Next semester, she's coming back with a Mercedes. She's been bragging about it all week. I'm throwing a brick through the window. That white satin rag she wore to the Peter Pan audition last year cost six thousand bucks. Six thousand, can you believe that? That's an actual fact, straight from Connie, and Connie knows because Connie was there when Karen whipped that Black American Express Card out and SWIPED it! And she'll never wear it again. Nobody's ever gonna see that thing again, because the next time there's an audition or a big formal party or whatever that credit card'll be sailin' over the skies of America again, and ol' Karen'll make her grand entrance in a sparkling new million dollar rag, which, worn once, will disappear like a plane in the Bermuda Triangle. Poof! The bitch must have a closet the size of the dining hall.

BRIAN. *(turning on a lamp)* Babe….

GAIL. Can you believe a Mercedes? She told me that herself. I think my mouth dropped open about two feet. Isn't she worried about driving a car like that in this city? Of course not, cause if something happens, like a scratch on the bottom of a tire, she'll just drive it to the nearest garbage dump and pick up another on the way home. It's not a problem.

BRIAN. Gail…

GAIL. What, honey?

BRIAN. The way you can go from sex to bitching in a lightning flash just really chills my blood.

GAIL. I'm not bitching.

BRIAN. You started before my tongue was even out of your mouth.

GAIL. Yeah?

BRIAN. And you're dressed now. Look at you. I can't believe it.

GAIL. Believe it. That cast list is goin' up any second, and I got better things to do than lay around all night.

BRIAN. I thought you didn't care about the cast list any more.

GAIL. I don't. I don't care. I stopped caring. Why should I care. I couldn't care less. The last show of my last year. A part I've wanted to play since I was four years old. The final theatrical production I have the potential of being involved with in my life, as long as I live, before I take my useless sixty thousand dollar diploma away to some shoe-box roach palace in the Bronx, wait on tables 'til I'm thirty, squirt the secret sauce on Big Macs 'til I'm forty, drop dead of fatigue when I'm fifty, why is there reason to CARE?!?!?

BRIAN. So then –

GAIL. Mickey's down there already. He's been there since noon. Didn't go to a class all day. You aware of that?

BRIAN. He wasn't in bio.

GAIL. Cause he was in the theatre sitting smack against the call board like a police dog. He missed Karlson's midterm and everything. I'm, you know why I'm telling you this? I'm telling you this so you can realize how incredibly calm and rational I'm being, considering.

BRIAN. Fine. Okay.

GAIL. I'm just telling you.

BRIAN. Great. Go, um, find out. Take your time. I've got things to do too.

GAIL. Because –

BRIAN. No more speeches, huh? If you keep babbling, my eardrums are gonna melt.

GAIL. Hey.

BRIAN. Well you just talk, and talk, you know. I don't even need to be in the room. You just go on, and on, from one subject to the next, it bothers me the way –

GAIL. – It bothers me the way I can't get a little support when I need it the most.

BRIAN. How can I support you? I can't get a word in! You're out in the sky some place, you and Mickey, man, runnin' around, makin' yourselves crazy over nothing –

GAIL. Nothing to you.

(She starts to leave.)

BRIAN. Babe, Gail, wait, okay –

GAIL. No, I'm –

BRIAN. Come on.

GAIL. What.

BRIAN. I'm sorry.

GAIL. You're –

BRIAN. Come over here.

GAIL. Brian, even as we speak, Karen Hedges is finding out she's been cast as Maria, and I think I need to be there to knock out a few of her teeth.

BRIAN. Well, when do I get a chance to be with you?

GAIL. You're with me now, we just –

BRIAN. I mean –

GAIL. We'll have all semester to spend together when I don't get cast.

BRIAN. You're cast. Don't pretend you think you're not. If not Maria, then some other part. Chorus, or –

GAIL. Oh. No. You do not seem to understand the situation, Brian –

BRIAN. Here we go.

GAIL. – because if they by some sick, unexplained mystery happen to get the guts to *dare* to stick me in that chorus after all I've done for them, my last show, it's – it's not as if –

BRIAN. Okay. I know. Okay.

GAIL. If it is such a hassle to listen to me –

BRIAN. It's not, Gail, if you say something new, I just can't take it any more, you should hear Mickey. He goes on and on just like you until three in the fucking morning. I go to sleep and have terrible nightmares about *West Side Story* and I'm not even in the theatre department.

GAIL. Do you dream I don't get Maria?

BRIAN. No, I dream that the Jets and the Sharks are dancing on top of my grave.

GAIL. Well, I guess I could get Maria. God knows I should get Maria. I don't think I'm being unrealistic about thinking I'm right for – I mean, poor Mickey. He honestly, *honestly* thinks he is right for Tony. I mean, I'm not being crazy, am I, to think –

BRIAN. What's the matter with Mickey playing Tony? He sounds okay –

GAIL. Babe, this is *West Side Story*. Not *La Cage*.

BRIAN. La what?

GAIL. Look. I don't have much going for me in this world, but I've at least got the capacity to be realistic when it comes to –

BRIAN. He was doin' that song in here the other day for the ten thousandth time and he sounds just like the guy on the CD.

GAIL. Trust me. They'd cast him as Anita before they give him Tony.

BRIAN. Well, then I don't understand, then.

GAIL. No. Ya don't.

BRIAN. I'm betting you both get the leads. You sing good together. You look good together.

GAIL. Standing next to him, I'm a ballerina hippo from *Fantasia*.

BRIAN. Well –

GAIL. But wait, can I just tell you about Karen Hedges' accent? Her Spanish accent? I mean, of course it's not a Spanish accent. Everyone who heard her read knew it wasn't a Spanish accent. What it was, what it is, that is a mystery no one can solve. Jack said she sounded like Miss Celie in The Color Purple. The point is, the hag has less acting talent than a rotten cantaloupe. But they don't care. They'll give her Maria. They've let her ruin enough shows at this school, what's one more, right?

BRIAN. *(His head is starting to throb.)* What's one more.

(He retreats to his desk and makes a thin attempt to get some work done.)

GAIL. Right. I mean, after she scared the living shit out of thousands of children as Peter Pan, you think they'd take a hint.

BRIAN. A hint.

GAIL. Kids were screaming. Crying, hysterical, all through the show. It was horrible. She just couldn't make them believe.

BRIAN. Horrible.

GAIL. And *Streetcar*. Jesus. She played that part like a deranged crack whore. Not that she could remember a single line –

BRIAN. Gail?

GAIL. Yes?

BRIAN. Why don't you go to the theatre now. I'm gonna try to get some stuff done.

GAIL. What did you wanna talk to me about?

BRIAN. It's not important.

GAIL. Later, maybe?

BRIAN. Later, you'll be incoherent. You'll be this big puddle of screeching goo.

GAIL. You're saying I won't get it?!?

BRIAN. You're saying you won't get it! What do I know? I'm just listening and agreeing because it's all I have the energy to do any more.

GAIL. I can't believe this. You really think I'm not good enough to play that part.

BRIAN. Oh my God. Gail. Honey. I know you could do it.

GAIL. Just *do* it?!

BRIAN. Do it great, amazing. Magnificent. Spectacular. The universe would never know a better performance… But –

GAIL. But?

BRIAN. Look, I just have this on my mind. I've got to say it to you.

GAIL. You think Karen Hedges would be better.

BRIAN. No, I don't think Karen Hedges would be better. Come over here and sit next to me.

GAIL. You've always had a little crush on her. You think I don't notice these things.

BRIAN. Would you give me two seconds please to say something to you?

(She sits next to him. She sits on an apple core. Stands up. Hands it to **BRIAN**.*)*

Ughhh, I'm sorry, this garbage pile I'm living in –

GAIL. *(sitting down again)* Every room is messy.

BRIAN. Some rooms are messy. This one's a landfill. *Mickey.* Look at this thing.

*(***BRIAN*** has picked up something disgusting.)*

Every day, I find a new, unidentified molding object. What is this?

GAIL. Brian, everyone's gonna know the list before I do.

BRIAN. I just wanna tell you something.

GAIL. If this is gonna be a relationship talk, how I'm a shitty girlfriend, blah blah –

BRIAN. I just wanna tell you one thing.

GAIL. One thing, huh?

BRIAN. One thing.

GAIL. Okay, lemme brace myself here.

BRIAN. You don't have to brace yourself for anything, Gail. I just wanna tell you that I love you.

GAIL. You love me.

BRIAN. I love you.

GAIL. You love me.

BRIAN. Yes.

GAIL. That's it?

BRIAN. And I love the time I spend with you.

GAIL. That's two things.

BRIAN. Oh. Sorry.

GAIL. Look. I'm…I'm sorry the way I act. I'm…uh…not a very good person.

BRIAN. What do you –

GAIL. Really, you know. Something inside of me is green and black and rotten. I can feel it there. I'm not good. I'm evil, sort of.

BRIAN. I've always wanted to date a demon.

GAIL. Well, it's true. Only an evil person would find joy thinking of Karen Hedges hanging upside down by her fake toenails from the top of the Empire State Building.

BRIAN. I'm sure many would find the same joy.

GAIL. As crazed and starving vultures peck out her eyeballs and send her entrails falling to Fifth Avenue.

BRIAN. Well –

GAIL. As she screams. I'm evil. I always felt sorry for the villains in Walt Disney movies when they fell over the cliff or got the dagger through their heart, whatever. The Queen in Snow White is a very sympathetic character. She's living her life, minding her own business, and along comes this sing-songy little bitch who prances around in a yellow hoops skirt talking to pigeons. I'm tellin' ya, I'd do the same thing the Queen did and order my guard to take her to the woods and rip her heart out.

BRIAN. Gail, I want you to get the part. I really do.

GAIL. So do I, boy, you know if –

BRIAN. Shhhhh…But um…part of me. Part of me is hoping you don't get it, that you don't even make the show. And wait a minute don't look at me like that, cause I wanna tell you why. Look, mmm…man. Okay. It's this. There's, the way I see it, there's these last few months of school left, and that's all I've got to spend with you before everything goes crashing into a black hole when who knows what's gonna happen to any of us, or anything. I've got a few ideas what might happen to you and me, but I don't like to think about 'em, cause they're not too happy. At least, I mean, I see what happens to like, Bob Carrera and Jodie. When Bob graduated, he met someone else two months later, and then Jodie did too and well…The way people zip through your life for a split second and then kaplow! Gone. It's safe here. It seems like it could go on forever, you and me. Until you get to the end of the track and the train goes spilling all the passengers over a cliff.

GAIL. We're not gonna –

BRIAN. No, we don't know what's gonna happen. I got another year left here, and you'll be out in the city making all your little theatre connections, that stuff, and then the train'll spit me out over the edge, but that's a year. By, by that time, I mean…who knows? I'm scared of what could happen to us, Gail. I know we aren't perfect, not even close to it, but losing friends and people I love makes me sick all through my body…But we've got these couple of months left. And we could have so much together, do so much, if…Well, if you had the time to spare. But you won't have it. You'll be in that theatre, every single night, every hour, every weekend, then…I'm, uh….I just love you, Gail. I'm sorry. I just love you and I'm scared. I'm sorry.

GAIL. Brian…It's not gonna end.

BRIAN. How can it not?

GAIL. We have to trust each other.

BRIAN. I do. I mean –

GAIL. But you don't understand how bad I want that part.

BRIAN. No, I do, and I want you to get it –

GAIL. You –

BRIAN. I do. I want you to get it. I'm being selfish to want anything else. This is your career. What's more important than that? It's what you came here for –

GAIL. But I love you –

BRIAN. And I love you. Look, this is stupid. Sometime I just feel as if, I don't know…I'm holding you back, something –

(**MICKEY** *enters, slamming the door. He is not happy. He is holding an empty tequila bottle, which he will promptly toss on the floor.*)

MICKEY. Don't ask me, I don't wanna talk about it. I need more liquor and I need it bad.

GAIL. Wait, don't tell me, I wanna look for myself!

BRIAN. It's up?

MICKEY. It *was* up til I ripped it down.

GAIL. Who's Maria?!?!?!?!? No!! Don't tell me! Is anyone there??

MICKEY. Everyone's there. Waiting for that bald headed stork Fergeson to type up a new list. The original is now floating somewhere in the New York sewage system.

GAIL. You ripped it down?! Seriously?!

MICKEY. I seriously did. And I seriously tore it into a hundred pieces and flushed it down the toilet. It is now exactly where it belongs. Floating with shit!!

GAIL. Who's Maria?!? I have to know! NO!! Don't say it, I can't stand it. Wait, who are you?

MICKEY. *(coy)* Me?

GAIL. You didn't get – ?

MICKEY. Darling, don't pretend you thought even for a moment that I *would* get Tony.

GAIL. Philip?

MICKEY. Who else?

GAIL. Oh my God, I can't believe he's –

BRIAN. *(holds up mystery object)* Mickey, what the hell is this?

MICKEY. A midnight snack.

GAIL. Did I make the show?!

MICKEY. You made it, all right.

GAIL. *(She has worked herself into complete hysterics.)* What's that supposed to mean? No! Don't tell me! I have to see for myself! Where's my other shoe?!?!

MICKEY. Yes, that's right. Don't concern yourself with my sorry fate, Gail. Friends like you –

GAIL. I'm concerned for you, Mickey, but you're not the only one at that audition who was up for a lead –

MICKEY. I may have been up for a lead, courtesy call that it was, but as of this moment, you may call me chorus boy number three.

GAIL. They didn't.

MICKEY. They nothing. Fergeson's the one who's gonna find new meaning in the word "terror" not long from now. My revenge shall be long and painful.

GAIL. I'm going now. I can't believe Philip. Jesus. I'm sorry, Mickey. Bye, Brian. I'll be back ten minutes, love you bye.

(She exits, slamming the door.)

MICKEY. Ohh, well. I never *really* thought I stood a chance against the North American Drug Connection.

*(**MICKEY** has picked up something, taken a bite, and tosses it on the floor halfway through **BRIAN**'s next line.)*

BRIAN. What the hell is that supposed to – PICK that up before I ram it straight up your ass!

MICKEY. Ooooh, you just gave me a hot flash.

BRIAN. Mickey, I want you to stop throwing your crap all over the floor. I can't walk to the bathroom at night with the lights out any more cause I'll step on the petrified remains of your last week's lunch!

MICKEY. Thanks, Brian. There's so much concern for my emotions at this college, I can barely stand it.

BRIAN. I can only be concerned about so much, okay? A person only has the ability to be concerned about so much before his brain splits into a million bloody shreds and explodes, what fuckin' part did you get this time?!

MICKEY. As if you care –

BRIAN. Well, Mickey, I better care, right, unless I want guilt for the next –

MICKEY. No, forget it.

BRIAN. What did Gail get?

MICKEY. I'm Nibbles.

BRIAN. Huh??

MICKEY. I never even knew there was a character in *West Side Story* named Nibbles, but there is, and I'm it, after all this build up, three lines, max. I'm sure, but hey, hey, hey, there's no small parts, only small actors, right?

BRIAN. I wouldn't know.

MICKEY. You wouldn't.

BRIAN. What'd Gail get?

MICKEY. See? You don't care about me, you don't care that I'm Nibbles, nobody cares that I'm Nibbles, it's my last show, I'm a goddamned Senior, they cast me as a character named Nibbles?!?!? Troy, you know Troy?

BRIAN. No.

MICKEY. Troy!! The freshman? The one with the teeth?! He's Chino! A FRESHMAN!!

BRIAN. Who's Chino?

MICKEY. Well he's a bigger godamned part than Nibbles!

BRIAN. Someone buy me a plane ticket to Siberia.

MICKEY. If it's such a hassle listening to me –

BRIAN. Were you and Gail separated at birth?!

MICKEY. An Engineering major could hardly understand.

BRIAN. I'm gonna lose it. I'm gonna scream 'til a lung flies outta my mouth. Mickey, I know you're all in a panic about this –

MICKEY. I'm not in any kind of a panic, I could care less, cast a drug addict as the fucking male lead. He's snorting up even as we speak. When he goes crashing off the fire escape on opening night in a cloud of white powder, they'll have only themselves to blame.

BRIAN. Listen, I hate –

MICKEY. Do you know that he can roll up a Kleenex tissue and put it in one nostril and pull it out through the other nostril?! The kid's note twenty-two and he's already snorted himself a third nostril!!

BRIAN. This room!!

MICKEY. I'll clean it. Forget it. Maybe I won't even do the show.

BRIAN. No, I can't forget –

MICKEY. Yes, you can, I mean, I have so many better things to worry about than getting on that stage and entertaining a bunch eighty year-old doctors and their families who are all too cheap to buy tickets to a Broadway show so they go see the magic of college theatre instead! All of 'em coughing and hacking and falling asleep at the most climactic moment of whatever's going on –

BRIAN. Mickey, it's enough, I wanna talk to you about this room.

MICKEY. *(spots a bottle of liquor, half-full)* Right here. This is what I need.

BRIAN. I can't live like this.

MICKEY. Jose Cuervo Gold. Come on, Brian. Let's do shots. Fly with me to Neverland!

BRIAN. No thanks, Lush, on a Tuesday night. Hey Mickey, it's getting really ridiculous in here. I feel like I'm living in a giant kitty box, except that the cats are shitting out pizza crust and half-Strawberry Pop-Tarts and mold covered peanut butter sandwiches!

MICKEY. I'll clean tomorrow. Can't you see I'm recovering from a tragic situation?

BRIAN. You got crap lying around from last semester! I finally got sick of staring at that green bagel and flushed it down the toilet. I'm surprised there wasn't an explosion!

MICKEY. All right, Joan. I'll clean tomorrow!

BRIAN. You won't, you say that, but –

MICKEY. Tomorrow, get off my back!

(**GAIL** *bursts back into the room.*)

GAIL. Okay! I can't take the suspense! Tell me!

MICKEY. *(slurping on the bottle, as he will continue to do for the rest of the play)* I ain't tellin' ya. Go look for yourself.

GAIL. I got halfway there, I couldn't see in front of me. I saw spots. Big, twirling orange and purple spots.

MICKEY. That means you have an aneurysm and you'll be dead within the hour.

GAIL. It's bad news, isn't it. It's Karen, isn't it? It is. You don't even have to say it, I see it in your – what? What are you smiling that way for?! Tell me before I –

MICKEY. It's you. You got it.

GAIL. I…what?! Got?!?

MICKEY. You –

GAIL. Don't play with me, Mickey, what, I got what, just say it, I'm telling you –

MICKEY. Maria.

GAIL. – to-huh-w-no, I did what? I got –

MICKEY. Maria. You got the part. You're Maria.

BRIAN. Mickey, what's the matter with you, why didn't you say something?!?

MICKEY.	**BRIAN.**
You got it.	Honey, that's fantastic!

GAIL. You're lying.

MICKEY. I'm gonna risk decapitation and lie about this, uh-huh –

GAIL. I'm Maria?!

BRIAN. Babe, Gail, this is –

GAIL. Oh, God, oh my God, oh, go-some-somebody get me a b-bag, I think I'm gonna –

MICKEY. Relax, bitch, it's what you always wanted.

GAIL. It's true? Mickey, it's really – wh-what are you?

MICKEY. I'm Nibbles.

GAIL. Oh God. I did it. I got it. What's Karen?

MICKEY. Some Jet girl, I don't remember.

BRIAN. Gail, I'm so happy for you.

GAIL. What?

MICKEY. Some dinky little –

GAIL. I'm Maria. Oh my God. I'm not – wait. I don't believe you.

MICKEY. Go see for yourself then.

GAIL. I'm going to.

MICKEY. Tequila?

BRIAN. Babe, come here, this is the best, it's –

GAIL. Yeah, right, I gotta, I hafta see this list right now. I'm Maria?!?

MICKEY. Yes, Gail, you are yes, Maria, and I am no, not Tony, and you could obviously not give a shit less.

GAIL.	MICKEY.
I'm gonna pass out, I think, I'm, God, is this possible, it's –	So what. Brian, don't we have some salt around here somewhere?

BRIAN. Huh?

GAIL. I'm Maria. I am Maria. Gail Kearson starring as Maria. Maria. Gail Kearson.

(GAIL goes insane. She leaps onto one of the beds and begins jumping up and down, screaming, hysterical, howling at the top of her lungs.)

BRIAN. *(as GAIL has her outburst)* What the hell are you doing? Get offa there. I already got thirty loose springs that stab me to death every night, I don't need – hey! Gail! Quit being an idiot –! It's great but –

GAIL. *(singing, jumping)* Maria—— the most beautiful sound I ever heard—— Maria—— Maria, Maria, Maria, Maria, Maria –

BRIAN. *(as she sings)* There, you did it! You hear that pop? That was a fresh spring popping! That was –

GAIL. *(leaps off the bed)* Maria———! I'll soon play a girl named Maria———! And Karen Hedges won't! I'll finally get what I deserve – ! Maria—— !

*(The door flies open and **KAREN** enters, full of nasty fury that is hidden below layers and layers of charm, smiles, and ease.)*

Maria——! Maria – Maria—— Maria – Maria – Mar –

*(She sees **KAREN** and freezes.)*

KAREN. Oh. Please. Don't stop.

GAIL. Karen –

KAREN. Such a lovely sound, after all.

MICKEY. C'mere, Karen, chug down some tequila with me.

KAREN. You're in so much trouble right now.

MICKEY. You jest.

KAREN. Ripping down the cast list like that. Of course, I can't say I blame you. In the least.

MICKEY. Something inside me just snapped.

KAREN. Didn't see you at the call-board, Gail.

GAIL. Didn't see me cause I wasn't there.

KAREN. Still, you know.

GAIL. I heard.

KAREN. Mmmm. Well, I just dropped by to say congratulations.

GAIL.	**MICKEY.**
Oh, w-thank, thank you, it Hasn't really sunk in yet –	So say it.

KAREN. And naturally, there are no hard feelings.

GAIL. Really? I mean, cause –

KAREN. I'm sure your performance will be quite astonishing.

GAIL. Ohhhuuh. Yeah. Ah, what role are *you* performing, Karen?

KAREN. I'm not. Ohh, they gave me some little consolation prize –

GAIL. Anita?

KAREN. A littler prize, Gail. Littler. But they surely know I can't possibly be bothered. They must realize.

GAIL. *(as* **KAREN** *pulls out a cigarette)* Please don't light up in here.

KAREN. *(crushes it, drops it onto the floor.)* And I'm glad, very glad the way things turned out. I never wanted Maria anyway.

GAIL. Well –

KAREN. Anyone'd have to be crazy. I'm saying that when you stop to think about the actual process that you're going to go through with Fergeson trying in vain to direct –

GAIL. Well, as I recall, Karen, you've never responded much to direction anyway –

BRIAN. *Anyway......*

KAREN. Oh, hello Brian. You're always so sweet and quiet.

BRIAN. All you theatre majors. Who can get a word in?

KAREN. Poor Brian, how lonely you'll be with Gail off emoting in the theatre every night –

BRIAN. I'm just glad she's finally getting her –

KAREN. *(more to* **GAIL** *than to* **BRIAN***)* Of course, I'll be around. Just down the hall.

MICKEY. Hun, what *Days of Our Lives* bitch are you tryin' to be?

KAREN. I just bought a new blender. I'll stop by every night. We'll have margarita parties.

GAIL. *(Not at all impressed. Just disgusted)* Karen, in four years, this is the *first* time you've "stopped by."

MICKEY. I'm playing Nibbles.

GAIL. What, you think you can make me nervous, jealous, you –

KAREN.	**GAIL.**
Jealous! God, no, I –	Cause believe me –

BRIAN. *(always the peace maker)* Come on, you guys, enough is –

KAREN. Jealous, Gail, please, just what do you think I am?

GAIL. Who cares what I think? You think you think you're a character from *Dynasy*!

KAREN. I'm only trying to be a good, um…loser about this, trying to –

GAIL. Christ, Karen, you've had three hundred parts at this school. This is my first lead, and my last for that matter. I mean come on, give me a break, huh?

MICKEY. Brian, let's call for a pizza.

GAIL. Don't act like you're any kind of a *loser*, Karen. If there's a loser here, it's me, all right? I wouldn't know what a spot light looks like!

KAREN. Well, I guess I shouldn't have bothered.

GAIL. Karen, you wanna play Maria so bad, just hock that dress you wore to the audition, you'll have enough cash to produce your very own revival!

KAREN. No, you know something, I honestly do not care.

GAIL. Honestly –

KAREN. You got it.

GAIL. Well –

KAREN. I mean, it was my part. Everyone knew that. As far as I'm concerned – no. I wouldn't dream of saying this to you.

GAIL. Please. Grace me with your wisdom.

KAREN. I don't think I should, because I have a little theory. Well – maybe it's more than theory. Maybe it's something I overheard Fergeson say just a very few days ago. It's my little theory of why you ended up with my – with that part.

BRIAN. Jesus Christ, it's just a show!

MICKEY. Best show they ever decided to do here, I say fight for it. Go on. Claw each other's eyes out. Let's see some blood!

GAIL. Fuck off, Mickey.

MICKEY. – tell me to fuck off in my own room, you gonna turn into this big diva monster now? It's happenin' already?!

GAIL. What's your theory, Karen?

KAREN. I don't think so.

GAIL. Y'know, I just have to laugh at you. At this, boy you are really – I can't even enjoy being successful one time, once, one time in four years?!? Gimme that bottle!

*(She yanks the bottle out of **MICKEY**'s hand, takes a big swig.)*

KAREN. I've wanted to play Maria since I was twelve.

GAIL. Well I've wanted to play her since I was four!

BRIAN. Oh for God's sake!

GAIL. And all the other parts you robbed from me! Blanche, and Reno Sweeney, and Annie Oakley, and, and –

MICKEY. Aldonza –

GAIL. Aldonza, yes! I could really relate to that part about being born on a dung heap!

KAREN. Really.

GAIL. Of course, you, with your diamond studded diapers –

MICKEY. How 'bout whatsername from *Barefoot in the Park* –

GAIL. *That* I could give a shit about –

MICKEY. Peter Pan –

GAIL. Peter Pan, don't get me started, how I wanted to play that role! And to see what you did with it, circling around like the Wicked Witch of the West – !

KAREN. Well, Gail, honey, if they'd tried to hoist your fat ass up on those ropes, the entire theatre would have caved in.

BRIAN.	**GAIL.**
All right already – !	What?!?

KAREN. Reality is –

GAIL. At least the kids wouldn't have gone home having to spend the rest of their lives in therapy! That letter the department got from the mother of that six year-old girl who thought you were the devil!

KAREN. Both newspapers raved.

GAIL. How much did you write the check for?

KAREN. You're an idiot.

GAIL. Because I –

KAREN. You don't have a clue.

BRIAN. You guys, this is really petty stuff here –

KAREN. But I think I might just give you one. A clue. As to why you are now a temporary star.

GAIL. Not that you could –

KAREN. Overheard conversations while at the theatre office copy machine are sometimes very revealing…very interesting. And something overheard recently was something concerning one Gail Kearson…Something, I believe, in a conversation between Fergeson and Jack Jacobs. Ohh, nothing too private. No major shockers. Just something about poor Gail Kearson, and how sad it is…Let's see. How did Fergeson phrase it? – "All that drive and energy in such a talentless body."

BRIAN. Get out of my room, Karen.

KAREN. I'm gone.

GAIL. You made that up.

KAREN. Connie heard it. Ask her. Yes, right from Fergeson's mouth. How sad…How badly she wants a lead. How she's tried for so long and yet she can't seem to display any more charisma than a tree stump. But such a hard worker and not a *bad* singing voice…just, now let me get this exactly right…I think it was – "A hopeless sort of nobody who deserves at least one moment in the spotlight…before a lifetime of rejection."

BRIAN. That's enough! What's wrong with you people?!? You all have switchblades stickin' outa your hearts?!? Get outa here, Karen, I mean it.

KAREN. It's true, Gail. I swear to God, I heard it said –

BRIAN. *(opening the door, using force)* Outa here, you stupid fuckin –

KAREN. Get off me! Ask Fergeson if you don't believe me! Ask Connie! She'll be glad to tell you! She wanted that part too!

(BRIAN has forced her from the room and now he slams the door in her face. She kicks the door hard, one time, and is gone. GAIL is destroyed. MICKEY is half crocked from slamming tequila, and is totally baffled. BRIAN doesn't know what to do or say. There is a long silence. BRIAN goes to GAIL.)

BRIAN. *(trying to laugh it off)* We-well, that sure was electrifying, huh? Hey, uh, uhm…You know, you're smart enough to know better than to believe anything that comes outa her mouth –

MICKEY. In her life she's told the truth maybe three times, Gail –

BRIAN. *(quickly pulls out his wallet, looks in, counts)* Hey, I got, twenty, thirty bucks here, we can't be si-sitting in, uh, here, on a night like this, right? Hey right?

MICKEY. Huh?

BRIAN. Come on, lemme just put on a, um, come on, we'll go down to Sanduskys, get some drinks –

MICKEY. I'll go.

BRIAN. – something to eat, uh, celebrate a little, you know –

MICKEY. Gail, quit brooding, if you think Fergeson'd give somebody a lead like Maria just outa pity, you must be really –

BRIAN. Mickey –

MICKEY. – and I mean anyway, it doesn't matter why they gave it to you. They gave it to you. It's yours. You. You. You. And now you get the rare and unexpected opportunity to show 'em all why they shoulda given you everything else, too.

BRIAN. You're getting all wound up again –

MICKEY. She's sittin' here like a jerk. At least she gets the chance. At least you get a chance to prove yourself, right. Right, Gail? What about me, huh? I'm a few months away from drowning in a swimming pool of loans, four years of thousands and thousands of dollars in student loans and what do I get outa those four years?!

BRIAN. Can ya just –

MICKEY. NIBBLES! I GET NIBBLES! If Nibbles has one line, ONE SOLITARY LINE in that play, I WILL FALL OFF THE STAGE IN AMAZEMENT!!!

GAIL. Wait a second...

MICKEY. *(keeps right on going)* But you, Gail, finally you –

GAIL. I really wish you wouldn't compare us, Mickey. You and me.

MICKEY. Honey, that ain't the point of what I'm –

GAIL. No, I really don't think you can stick the two of us in a sen–, in the same sentence like that okay. I don't think it's fair, I don't, and I don't appreciate it, so just sit there, Mickey. Just sit on your bed and shut up.

MICKEY. I was trying to make you feel better.

GAIL. Don't. I feel better. I never felt better. Nobody has to make me feel anything at all, I'm not a complete fool, get it? I know how bitter she is, can I blame her? I don't blame her at all. She'd say anything to ruin-just to make herself feel–, Mickey just don't lump yourself together with me, don't do it! We're different!

MICKEY. Different.

GAIL. You got it. I got reality going for me, which is a word you've never quite been able to understand. If you – let me tell you – if you're gonna have the slightest chance of success in this business, you better get a grip Mickey, on, on what parts you're right for and what you –

MICKEY. I have a *grip*, Gail. Do you?

GAIL. You think you're right for every lead that comes along, Mickey, and maybe it's time for you to look in the mirror and –

MICKEY. I don't think that, Gail. I hope it…I wish it…forget it.

(**MICKEY** *gets up to leave.*)

BRIAN. Where in hell do you think you're going?

MICKEY. In search of alcohol.

BRIAN. You drained that whole bottle??

MICKEY. Tasted like water to me.

BRIAN. You're smashed. Get back here, we'll order a pizza –

MICKEY. Gail…I know I may not be right for many parts. I play dumb, maybe try to fool myself a little but I'm not a complete fool either. Gail…I know I wasn't right for Tony. They'd never think of handing me a lead like that. So what. Maybe I've wasted…maybe I'll never… but I can wish…I can hope…I can try. And so, I will.

(*He stares at her for a moment, and then exits quietly.*)

BRIAN. Christ, now he's gonna go jump off a roof.

GAIL. He'll be fine. He'll end up in Connie's room talkin' shit behind my back.

BRIAN. Well…you wanna, um, we can still go get something to eat.

GAIL. Brian?

BRIAN. Yeah?

GAIL. Is it true?

BRIAN. …is it, what?

GAIL. I just, I always believe you when you tell me how, how good I am, how much talent I have. I believe you because you promise me you're being honest –

BRIAN. Babe –

GAIL. Well, are you? Are you being honest, the things you say?

BRIAN. It's what you want to do with your life.

GAIL. So you tell me that I have the best voice in the department, and I'm gonna one day be on Broadway and all the other crap that pours out of your mouth every minute of the day, what is that? Lies?!

BRIAN. I love you, Gail.

GAIL. You love me, you love me. How?! Is there one loveable aspect about my personality?!

(She collapses on a bed, and tears come quickly.)

BRIAN. …Hey…Gail…hey…stop, it's okay.

GAIL. You don't have to love me any more. I'm just a self-absorbed hack who can't even –

BRIAN. Shhhhh, stop bein' crazy –

GAIL. I don't give you anything. All I care about it –

BRIAN. Stop, I'm not gonna listen to that. You're all worked up over nothing. It's okay. You're the most beautiful person I've ever known. I could never love anyone more.

GAIL. …How…can I know if I'm good enough?

BRIAN. You're more than that. You're the most talented, most beautiful – you sound just like the girl on the CD when you sing that –

GAIL. That's the same thing you said about Mickey.

BRIAN. Huh?

GAIL. That's the same thing you said, that's the same thing you said about Mickey. And it's not true with him. How can I believe you when you say the same thing to me?

BRIAN. Because I love you, Gail.

GAIL. So that makes a lie okay?!

BRIAN. Yes! No! I'm not lying, I mean –

GAIL. I don't care. I don't care if you're lying, or if you're not. I don't care what Fergeson thinks, or Connie, or Jack Jacobs, or Karen Hedges, and her thousand dollar dress. I have it inside of me to be better than anyone else. This is my turn in the spotlight, and I feel it, a hot white light. Around me, inside me until it's right there next to the green black ugly part of me, but this is bigger. Stronger. And when that light starts growing, it burns the green black part away until there's nothing left of it. The ugly part is gone and inside me, my body is alive with hot, white fire. The light is all around me, and everyone knows that I'm good. The rest of the stage is black. I'm in a pool of fire, and everybody loves me. What other ecstasy can there be than when thousands of people are loving you all at once. It's my turn, now. And it's all I've ever wanted.

BRIAN. ……and where do I fit into that…?

GAIL. …Will you hold me…?

BRIAN. I'll never stop.

GAIL. I'm scared.

BRIAN. So am I, Gail.

GAIL. Do you lie to me?

BRIAN. I love you.

GAIL. Do you lie to me?

BRIAN. I just love you, Gail.

GAIL. *(laughs a little, through teary eyes)* W…well…It almost sounds like I have my answer…

*(**BRIAN** holds her close. He is silent.)*

Well go on then….tell me a story…make me feel better.

*(**BRIAN** pauses for a long moment. The lights begin to slowly fade away.)*

BRIAN. ……………You sound better than the girl on the CD….You have the best voice at this school….One day you're gonna be famous, and rich enough to make Karen Hedges look like a bag lady……I know just where I fit into your life….We're gonna make it….and everything will be all right.

(The lights fade to black.)

The End

**Also by
Buddy Thomas...**

The Crumple Zone

Devil Boys from Beyond

Physical

Please visit our website **samuelfrench.com** for complete descriptions and licensing information.

OTHER TITLES AVAILABLE FROM SAMUEL FRENCH

THE CRUMPLE ZONE

Buddy Thomas

Full Length, Comedy / 5m / Int.

This hilarious off Broadway hit, set in a run down apartment on Staten Island, concerns three gay roommates coming to crisis during one frantic Christmas weekend. Terry, an out of work actor who can't keep a job or get a date, spends his days swilling cheap vodka and playing referee to a messy love triangle. Extremely funny and deeply moving, *THE CRUMPLE ZONE* is about staying together, breaking apart and the things we lose along the way.

"The kind of domestic comedy that might have been written by Neil Simon if he were gay and 40 years younger!"
– *The New York Times*

"A little gem."
– Liz Smith

"Guaranteed to keep the laughter in overdrive!"
– *New York Daily News*

"Sparkles! The first fresh comedy of its type to come along in years. It is not going too far to draw parallels between Neil Simon or Kaufman & Hart at the top of their powers.... A rollicking farce with a heart of pure gold."
– *LGNY Newspaper*

OTHER TITLES AVAILABLE FROM SAMUEL FRENCH

DEVIL BOYS FROM BEYOND

Buddy Thomas and Kenneth Elliott
Based on an original script by Buddy Thomas
Original song, *Sensitive Girl*, music and lyrics by Drew Fornarola

Comedy / 4m, 4f (all female roles can be played by men in drag) / Unit Set

**Winner! 2009 FringeNYC Overall Excellence Award for Outstanding Play!
Nominee! 2010 GLAAD Award for Outstanding New York Theater:
Off-Off Broadway!**

Flying Saucers! Backstabbing Bitches! Muscle Hunks and Men in Pumps! Wake up and smell the alien invasion in this outrageous comedy by the author of the off-Broadway hit play, *Crumple Zone*

"***** [FIVE STARS]! Buddy Thomas's deliriously campy sci-fi spoof—one of the most entertaining shows I have ever seen at the Fringe Festival—is naughty, gleeful fun…The show opens a fabulous portal to the past: not just the paranoid world of the 1950s, but the legendary drag romps of Charles Ludlam's Ridiculous Theatrical Company and Charles Busch's Theatre-in-Limbo from the 1960s through the 1980s. *Devil Boys from Beyond* is a necklace of golden links to that wild theatrical tradition. If there were any justice in this mixed-up world of ours, the whole show would be tractor-beamed Off Broadway tomorrow."
– Adam Feldman, *Time Out New York*

"Cheap in all the right ways, the fast, taw dry and very funny *Devil Boys From Beyond* is the Fringe Festival at its best."
– *New York Post*

"The larger-than-life homage to leading ladies and low-budget sci-fi films of the '50s…The audience's enthusiastic reception…guaranteed you'll laugh your anal probe off."
– *NYTheatre.com*

SAMUELFRENCH.COM

OTHER TITLES AVAILABLE FROM SAMUEL FRENCH

PHYSICAL

Buddy Thomas

Full Length, Comedy / 2m, 2f / Int.

It is the coldest night in November. Owen has shelved his college books and thesis papers to prepare for the date of his life. With candlelight, soft music and enough Italian chicken to feed the Northeast coast, he is ready but not for Aurora, the drugstore cosmetics cashier he has finally had the courage to ask for a date. All lipstick and hair spray and spike heels, Aurora is a combination of every cover girl in the history of Cosmopolitan, but her brain is made of paper too. Nothing goes as planned. When Aurora falls for Owen's roommate, things really get out of hand. Throw in Frieda, a psycho obsessive neighbor who has weddings with Barbie dolls and wields a mean butcher knife, and you have a physical comedy of lunatic proportions. Note: Includes numerous great monologues and scenes.

OTHER TITLES AVAILABLE FROM SAMUEL FRENCH

BIFF AND CHARLIE

Chambers Stevens

Comedy, TYA and High Schools / 1m, 1f / Interior

Biff and Charlie takes place at the Andrew Jackson Performing Arts High School in Nashville, TN. Biff, an accomplished pianist, is rehearsing his audition pieces for Julliard when theatre student Charlie, dressed as Henny Penny, runs in hiding from her children's theatre director. This mismatched couple soon start dating. Mozart, prom, sexual awakening and a dog who should have looked where he was going teaches our young couple that first love is lot more challenging that it looks.

SAMUELFRENCH.COM

OTHER TITLES AVAILABLE FROM SAMUEL FRENCH

OFF OFF BROADWAY FESTIVAL PLAYS, 34TH SERIES

Various Authors

One of Manhattan's most established play festivals, the Samuel French Off Off Broadway Short Play Festival fosters the work of emerging writers, giving them the exposure of publication and representation.

The festival resulting in this collection was held July 14th-19th, 2009 at The Main Stage Theatre on 42nd Street in New York City.

From the initial pool of over 715 submissions, the Final Forty plays were chosen to be performed over a period of one week. A panel of judges comprised of celebrity playwrights, theatrical agents and artistic directors nominated one or more of each evening's plays as finalists. The final round was then held on the last day of the festival. Out of these plays, six winners listed below were chosen by Samuel French, Inc. to receive publication and licensing contracts.

Winning plays and playwrights for this collection include:

Drop by J. Michael DeAngelis and Pete Barry
The Education Of Macoloco by Jen Silverman
realer than that by Kitt Lavoie
The Student by Matt Hoverman
Thucydides by Scott Elmegreen and Drew Fornarola
Just Knots by Christina Gorman

SAMUELFRENCH.COM

OTHER TITLES AVAILABLE FROM SAMUEL FRENCH

SKIN DEEP

Jon Lonoff

Comedy / 2m, 2f / Interior Unit Set

In *Skin Deep*, a large, lovable, lonely-heart, named Maureen Mulligan, gives romance one last shot on a blind-date with sweet awkward Joseph Spinelli; she's learned to pepper her speech with jokes to hide insecurities about her weight and appearance, while he's almost dangerously forthright, saying everything that comes to his mind. They both know they're perfect for each other, and in time they come to admit it.

They were set up on the date by Maureen's sister Sheila and her husband Squire, who are having problems of their own: Sheila undergoes a non-stop series of cosmetic surgeries to hang onto the attractive and much-desired Squire, who may or may not have long ago held designs on Maureen, who introduced him to Sheila. With Maureen particularly vulnerable to both hurting and being hurt, the time is ripe for all these unspoken issues to bubble to the surface.

"Warm-hearted comedy … the laughter was literally show-stopping. A winning play, with enough good-humored laughs and sentiment to keep you smiling from beginning to end."
- TalkinBroadway.com

"It's a little Paddy Chayefsky, a lot Neil Simon and a quick-witted, intelligent voyage into the not-so-tranquil seas of middle-aged love and dating. The dialogue is crackling and hilarious; the plot simple but well-turned; the characters endearing and quirky; and lurking beneath the merriment is so much heartache that you'll stand up and cheer when the unlikely couple makes it to the inevitable final clinch."
- NYTheatreWorld.Com

SAMUELFRENCH.COM

www.ingramcontent.com/pod-product-compliance
Lightning Source LLC
Chambersburg PA
CBHW070651300426
44111CB00013B/2364